FUNDAMENTALS

GO

FUNDAMENTALS

EVERYTHING YOU NEED TO KNOW TO PLAY AND WIN ASIA'S MOST POPULAR GAME OF MARTIAL STRATEGY

by Shigemi Kishikawa

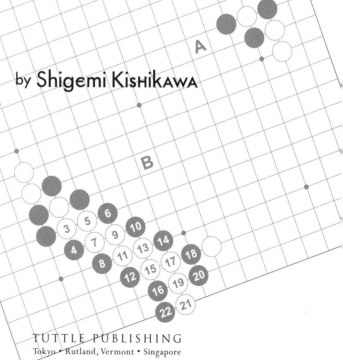

TUTTLE PUBLISHING
Tokyo • Rutland, Vermont • Singapore

Published by Tuttle Publishing, an imprint of Periplus Editions (HK) Ltd., with editorial offices at 364 Innovation Drive, North Clarendon, Vermont 05759 U.S.A.

Library of Congress Cataloging-in-Publication Data

Kishikawa, Shigemi.
  Go fundamentals / by Shigemi Kishikawa.
    p. cm.
  ISBN 978-4-8053-1070-0 (pbk.)
1. Go (Game) I. Title.
  GV1459.5.K56 2009
  794'.4--dc22
                              2009013580

ISBN 978-4-8053-1070-0

Distributed by

North America, Latin America & Europe
Tuttle Publishing
364 Innovation Drive
North Clarendon, VT 05759-9436 U.S.A.
Tel: 1 (802) 773-8930; Fax: 1 (802) 773-6993
info@tuttlepublishing.com
www.tuttlepublishing.com

Japan
Tuttle Publishing
Yaekari Building, 3rd Floor
5-4-12 Osaki, Shinagawa-ku
Tokyo 141 0032
Tel: (81) 3 5437-0171; Fax: (81) 3 5437-0755
tuttle-sales@gol.com

Asia Pacific
Berkeley Books Pte. Ltd.
61 Tai Seng Avenue #02-12
Singapore 534167
Tel: (65) 6280-1330; Fax: (65) 6280-6290
inquiries@periplus.com.sg
www.periplus.com

13 12 11 10 09   6 5 4 3 2 1

Printed in Singapore

TUTTLE PUBLISHING® is a registered trademark of Tuttle Publishing, a division of Periplus Editions (HK) Ltd.

Contents

Foreword 7

Introduction 15

CHAPTER 1   Equipment 17

CHAPTER 2   The Game 21

CHAPTER 3   Territory 29

CHAPTER 4   Connection and Disconnection 33

CHAPTER 5   Capture 39

CHAPTER 6   Life and Death 49

CHAPTER 7   Illegal Plays 65

CHAPTER 8   Seki Situation 69

CHAPTER 9   Ko Situation 75

CHAPTER 10 Basic Tactics 81

CHAPTER 11 Playing the Game 97

Problems 103

Solutions 115

The End of the Game 127

Foreword

The first substantive knowledge of the Chinese game of go in the in the western world dates from 1687, when the young Chinese scholar Shen Fuzong explained the game to Thomas Hyde at the Bodleian Library in Oxford, England. Shen, brought to Europe by a Jesuit missionary, had already been paraded at the Versailles court where the Sun King Louis requested a demonstration of chopsticks—but on gold plates, naturally.

Although Hyde was alert to the merits of the game and wrote about it, he clearly had only a fuzzy grasp of it, and go caught on in Europe no more than did chopsticks.

It was not until the self-imposed isolation of Japan was breached by Commodore Perry's "black ships" in the mid 19th century and westerners began flocking there that its devotees learned enough to play an actual game and to teach others. Go had reached Japan from China over a thousand years before, and had been developed into its "national game." A tiny handful of westerners even became tolerably proficient. The most notable was the chemist Oskar Korschelt, who studied at the school of the top player, Honinbo Shuho. He got to within a six-stone handicap of Shuho. On his return to Germany, Korschelt, who found "exceptional pleasure" in studying Shuho's openings, shared his delight on the game with his 1884 work *Das "Go"-Spiel*. In itself, this was probably the single most important work that introduced the game to the west, but it had added importance in that it was heavily used by Arthur Smith for his *Game of Go*. This latter work had the advantage of being in English and published (by Tuttle, be it noted) in the large market of America.

Smith's book was the one I learned from, also with exceptional pleasure. It is still a worthy book, but dated. It is not just that the references to players and openings are out of date, but that the rules are now a little different.

Despite all the merits of the Korschelt and Smith books, the plain fact was that in their heyday go was still a fringe activity in the west. There were a few clubs, but next to no materials for teaching beyond the beginner stage, and for most players just getting equipment to play on was a major problem. Many players of my generation, myself included, began by using makeshift boards with confectionary or drawing pins for the pieces.

The transition to the modern position of the game, where go is played widely outside the Far East, with a massive number of clubs and tournaments, well over 200 non-beginner books in English and a profusion of cheap equipment, did not begin until around 1960.

The first edition of this book, then called *Stepping Stones to Go*, was an important part of that movement.

Buoyed up by its people's spectacular post-war economic recovery, the Japanese government began a concerted campaign of garnering goodwill overseas. Go was part of the drive. The go professionals' organisation, the Nihon Ki-in, was encouraged to start a magazine in English, to send professionals abroad to teach, and to hold international tournaments for amateurs. Many Japanese amateurs such as Kishikawa also made strenuous efforts to share their beloved game with new western friends.

The movement was so successful that nowadays go is no longer seen as a strange game in the west. Figures are loosely bandied around but the most conservative claim is that there are about 27 million regular players in the world with about 5 million of those outside the Far East. Around 60 countries participate in the World Amateur Championship that has been held annually in Japan since 1979 (there were sporadic events before that), and over 600 players, professional and amateur, played go in the first World Mind Sports Games, held in conjunction with the Olympics in Beijing in 2008.

The Japanese government's efforts to foster go were not limited to the west. Top players from China, Taiwan, and Korea were allowed to become professionals in Japan, and there were also high-level goodwill exchanges, especially in China where the game had languished somewhat throughout the upheavals of the 20th century. Naturally, the aim was to promote international relations rather than the game, but here too success was great. Even in the last few months of when I write, while politicians and newspapers talked of stalled arms talks with "evil" North Korea, ordinary North Koreans were mixing with go players of other nations in the WMSG and events in Japan. Proof yet again that even if chess is a game of war, go is a game of co-existence.

To a degree it could be said that the Japanese drive was too successful. At least, the top players in the world are now considered to be Korean (for example, Lee Changho and Lee Sedol), or Chinese (Gu Li and Chang Hao). A further characteristic has been the extreme youth of the Korean and Chinese players. Lee Changho (born in 1975) won his first world championship at the age of 16.

But in many ways go remains stronger in Japan than elsewhere. There is more money in go there, more professionals, more events, more books, more magazines. And although official efforts to spread the game overseas have eased off, it is the long-running Japanese manga (comic) *Hikaru no Go* which has brought in a massive new generation of young people into the game in recent years in both east and west.

What I am driving at is that, despite the prominence of Korean and Chinese players at the top, much of go in the west still bears the stamp of Japanese influence, both historical and modern. It is still a good idea to learn from a book by a Japanese author.

The rules that most western people are familiar with are Japanese. (Chinese rules differ slightly but Korean rules are the same as Japanese). Japanese terms such as ko, joseki, fuseki, aji, and hane are in wide use among western players, whereas no Chinese or Korean terms have made the grade

So the advice in this proven primer, *Go Fundamentals*, remains as valid as ever it was. More so in that it is now much easier to find equipment, opponents and tournaments. In the USA the best starting point is the American Go Association, http://www.usgo.org/. In Europe, where every country has its own association, a good starting point is the European Go Federation site, http://www.eurogofed.org/. Outside these areas the go wiki encyclopaedia Sensei's Library http://senseis.xmp.net/ will guide you to the relevant organisations. If you need to ask questions, the moderated forum http://www.godiscussions.com/ is your best port of call.

Once you can play, you can also find many opponents worldwide, of any strength, through online games on the internet. Most westerners seem to play on KGS at http://www.gokgs.com/ though there are several other servers (Sensei's Library has all the advice you need for these). Note that Japanese rules are the norm on the servers.

How far can you go if you learn in the west? Well, there are now western professionals. Michael Redmond from San Francisco has reached the top rank of 9-dan in Japan. Alexandre Dinerchtein of Russia is a professional 3-dan in Korea and Joanne Missingham from Australia (but living in San Diego since 2004) qualified as a professional in China in 2008. There are also professionals living in the west, though their income here is from teaching rather than tournaments. Some are western born. Some are from the respective professional organisations in the Far East, despatched here on long-term goodwill missions. All these can be contacted via the sites mentioned above.

But even without striving to reach professional standard, you will be learning a game that puts you in intimate contact with some 2,000 years of Asian history and culture. It is a game that has been prized there above all other games for its ability to teach reasoning, self-discipline, creativity. It has long been associated with officials, scholars, and poets in China, as *weiqi*. Their most beloved poet Du Fu is only one of hundreds that have left us go poems, and every major novel from ancient China is replete with references to the game. In Japan the author of the *Tale of Genji*, Murasaki Shikibu was a splendid player, and mentions the game many times in her 11th century novel. Her contemporary, Sei Shonagon, was also a strong player and mentions go in her *Pillow Book*. The samurai played go, but not as a game of war. From around 1600 the samurai may have been technically obliged to keep up their military training but in practice were mostly officials, and go was seen as a way of making them more, not less, civilized. In Korea, too, go, known as *baduk*, has long been the game of aristocrats and scholars, though until modern times they played a version known as *sunjang baduk*, still on a 19x19 board but with some starting stones and a different way of counting. Tibet still has a 17x17 version, with rather different rules, that is becoming a centerpiece of efforts to promote tourism in Shangri-la. Go tourism is also burgeoning in Japan and Korea.

Even beyond history and culture, go has things to teach us. With a world champion at the age of 16, it will be evident that strong players begin very early in the Far East. Five-year-olds are not unusual. How do they do it? There is no equivalent of our soccer moms and tennis dads. The most usual process in the Far East is for a promising player to go to live with a teacher. Rather than learn direct from the teacher, the child usually learns by playing with other children. Somehow or other, this system produces not just strong players but individuals who are well educated and well balanced. Not every child becomes a professional, of course, but that does not imply failure. Given the high intellectual status of the game for centuries, even just becoming a very strong player has benefits. In modern China, for example, proficiency in go is one way to beat the intense competition to land a place at an elite university.

At the other end of the spectrum, go has apparently been shown to provide beneficial intellectual stimulation that aids in staving off senile diseases. This may (like many of its benefits) be because it is a game that relies heavily on pattern recognition rather than pure analysis—right brain over left brain. In any event, there have been some remarkable stories. In 2006, Wada Kosaku, a former member of the Japanese Diet, being a 6-dan amateur (normally the highest grade of amateur) decided to treat himself, as a birthday present, to a game with a professional 9-dan. He lost by only 12 points with a four-stone handicap. It was his 99th birthday. But he was already a strong player. Not long before that, an amateur in Hokkaido *reached* the grade of 6-dan at the age of 100.

So go already offers us a mass of ways to enrich our lives apart from just placing pieces on a board. Yet there is still another facet that can make the game especially valuable for western players. Although go has traditionally been seen as one of the liberal arts in Asia, it has mostly appealed in the west to players who have some sort of background in mathematics or computing. The reaction of a fair number of these people to go can be seen in that of former world chess champion Emanuel Lasker. Intrigued by the game, he was nevertheless convinced that he and his friends could eventually match the Japanese masters through application of logic and analysis. In fact, he never got to within a nine-stone handicap (rather like queen odds in chess). But it is my experience that, once the shock wears off, such players become even more intrigued by go and realise it has new things to teach them. They are learning for themselves the exhortation of Confucius, from over 2,000 years ago, that one should "renew oneself day by day" Go has often been used as a model of that famous saying, because one aspect of it that fascinated even the ancients is that it is a game of infinite variety—the same game never appears twice.

But, if you prefer, there is no need to be philosophical about the game. The most significant fundamental of go is that it is just plain fun.

John Fairbairn
London, 2009

Introduction

Go is a game played by two contestants. The game is played with black and white "stones" on a checkered board. The players are usually classed as strong and weak, based upon degree of knowledge and skill. The stronger player takes the white stones and the weaker player takes the black stones. Handicaps are given the weaker players by mutual agreement before commencement of the game. The game of go may be one of the most difficult to learn, but this fact makes the game highly interesting. Once techniques are mastered, the beginner will find it difficult to put the game aside.

Now, let's learn how to play go in the following chapters.

CHAPTER 1
Equipment

The board or *go ban*

The board, or *go ban* as it is called in Japanese, is a solid block of wood, generally about four or five inches thick, resting upon four detachable legs. It is about 17½ inches long and 16 inches wide. The board and legs are usually stained yellow.

The best boards are made of *kaya* (*Torreya Nucifera*, or the famous Torrey pine of California). However, these boards are extremely expensive. Boards are also made of *katsura* (Japanese Judas tree), *icho* (gingko), or *hinoki* (Japanese cypress). *Katsura* boards, reasonable in price, are the most widely used today. Recently, flat boards without legs have been introduced, and are popular because they are more convenient and suitable when the game is played on a table or in a similar position.

The board is crisscrossed by 19 vertical and 19 horizontal lines, forming 361 points of intersection, and there are nine dotted points on its surface. These are called *hoshi* which means star, and they are used by the weaker player in the event of a handicap game. As will be seen, this gives the weaker player an advantage. Diagram 1 shows the surface of a *go ban*.

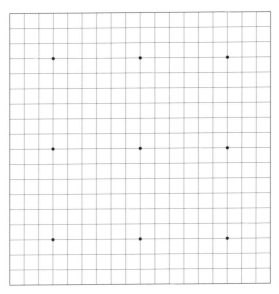

Diagram 1

The surface of go ban showing the nine dotted points called hoshi

The stones or *go ishi*

As mentioned above, there are two kinds of stones: white and black. The white stones are made from clamshells that come from Miyazaki Prefecture in Kyushu, the southern part of Japan. They have a lustrous polish and are pleasant to the touch. The black stones are made of a special kind of stone from the Nachi cataract in Kishiu, in central Japan, and are called Nachi *ishi*. As a good set of stones is quite expensive, cheaper stones, made of hard glass, are widely utilized. There are 361 stones, corresponding to the number of the points of intersection on the board. One hundred and eighty are white and the remaining 181 are black. As the weaker player takes the black stones and is entitled to the first move, the extra stone is black. In actual play, about 150 stones of each color are sufficient to play a game. The stones are contained in lacquered boxes or *go ke*.

The stones in play are placed on the points of intersection of the lines and *not* on the squares as in chess. Once placed, they cannot be removed, remaining on the points where they are placed until the end of a game, except when they are captured.

A hint should be given the beginner not to grasp a large handful of stones in one hand and use it to feed the other. Each stone should be withdrawn from the box at the conclusion of the opponent's turn to play and only when it is required for immediate use.

It is not absolutely necessary to learn the correct way to handle stones, but, for your reference, it is as follows: grasp the stone lightly between middle and index fingers of the right hand, resting it lightly on the nail of the index finger—an act that requires some practice to perform gracefully.

CHAPTER 2

The Game

The object of the game

The object of go is to secure territory as represented by the number of the unoccupied points of intersection. At the end of the game, the amount of vacant space is calculated, and the stones that have been captured are used to fill up the vacant spaces claimed by the opponent. The winner is the player who has succeeded in occupying the larger territory after the captured stones are used in this way.

With this ultimate object in view, two plans of action are followed, one being simply to rail off space by forming walls of stones around the area which the player desires to occupy, and the other that of capturing the stones or space of the opponent. However, if the players merely fence in parts of the board regardless of each other's play, a dull and monotonous game results. More interesting games develop when the players, in their efforts to secure territory, attack each other's stones or space, as will be explained later. The game is concluded when neither player is able to secure further unoccupied territory and when neither is willing to hazard further attacks on the territory already surrounded by his opponent.

The rules of play

Black plays first, placing one of his stones on any intersection on the board. Thereafter Black and White play alternately.

Aside from some rules relating to specific situations (explained later), all the necessary basic rules to play go are as follows:

1. The board must be so placed that the narrow sides are immediately opposite each player.

2. The stones are played on the points of intersection of the lines. As mentioned in Chapter 1, once placed they are not moved except when captured or for counting purposes at the end of the game.

3. With evenly matched players, the right of first move is decided by having one player hold a handful of stones and his opponent calling odd or even. If the opponent guesses correctly, he wins the black stones, and has the advantage of playing first.

4. When players are not evenly matched, the weaker player is given a handicap and he uses the black stones. In this case, White has the first move, and Rule 3 is ignored.

5. When all of the intersections adjacent to a stone or a group of stones are occupied by stones of the opponent, that stone or group of stones is captured and removed from the board.

6. It is forbidden to play on any point which is completely surrounded by the opponent's stones and there is only the one point vacant, unless the play results in the capture of all or part of the surrounding stones, because no stone may remain on the board if it is completely surrounded by stones of the opposite color.

7. If a group of stones contains two separate "eyes" (explained in detail in Chapter 6), it is permanently safe from capture, regardless of the enemy stones surrounding the group.

8. In a *ko* position (described in detail in Chapter 9), a player cannot repeat his previous move without first playing at some other part of the board.

9. To arrive at the final score, White counts the points within Black's territory and Black counts White's. To facilitate counting, the respective territories should be arranged as far as possible in rows of tens and twenties. Stones may be transferred from one place to any other place for this purpose.

Observers are not supposed to make comments. Even nowadays boards with four legs have a hollow on the reverse side in which in olden times the gory head of the interfering bystander was placed as a hint to others.

It is usually considered impolite to make the first move upon the central point of the board except in handicap games. At the end of the game, the stones should be returned to each player and not left in position.

Although not a part of the rules of the game, it seems appropriate here to describe briefly the purpose of handicaps. Before commencing play, handicaps are given by the stronger player in order to equalize the game between the two contestants. The placing of handicaps is shown in Diagrams 2-9.

Though only nine points are marked on the board, handicaps of 13, 17, and even 21 are given by advanced players to beginners. However, handicaps larger than nine stones are seldom practicable. Therefore, the nine-stone handicap is ordinarily the recognized maximum.

In the beginning, progress at playing go is very rapid, and handicaps are reduced very quickly. Usually, four, or sometimes three, wins cause a decrease of one stone in the handicap allowed. When handicaps are given, Black loses his right to first move since he has the advantage of stones already on the board.

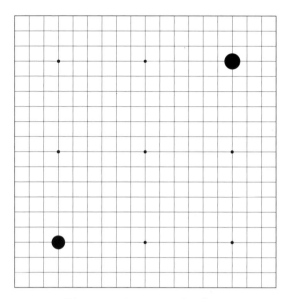

Diagram 2 A two-stone handicap

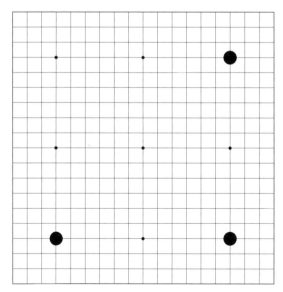

Diagram 3 A three-stone handicap

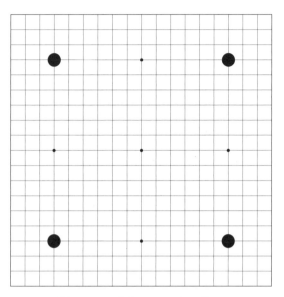

Diagram 4 A four-stone handicap

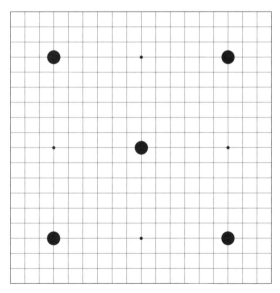

Diagram 5 A five-stone handicap

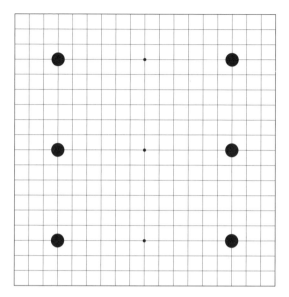

Diagram 6 A six-stone handicap

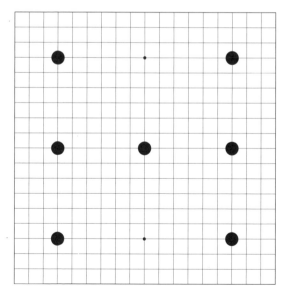

Diagram 7 A seven-stone handicap

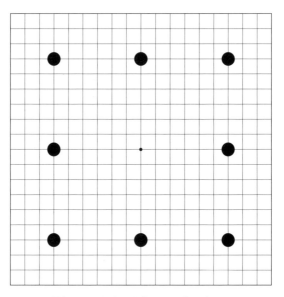

Diagram 8 An eight-stone handicap

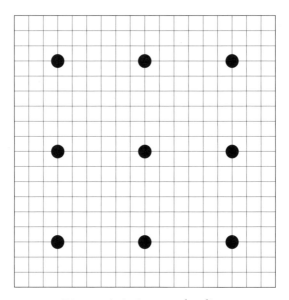

Diagram 9 A nine-stone handicap

CHAPTER 3
Territory

In the preceding chapter you learned that the primary object of go is to secure territory with your stones. The vacant areas surrounded by the players' stones are called territories, and each point of intersection is counted as one point in the possessor's favor. Let's study the diagram on the following page.

Each of the vacant areas surrounded by the four groups of stones in Diagram 10 is territory belonging to Black and White respectively. The two White groups have 25 points of territory and the two Black groups have 19 points of territory. Thus, it is apparent that the territory is the area which is completely surrounded by connected stones of the same color. In actual games, a number of independent territories like these is usually formed by each contestant. Diagram 11 shows another typical form of territory, although it is far from any actual game. It may seem to you that White's territory in the center of the board is larger than that of Black who controls the outside area of the board, but it is not because Black has 140 points of intersection (the entire outer border), and White has only 121 points of intersection. The diagram indicates that acquiring territory on the corners is most important since it can be secured more easily than any other place and with less stones. This will be explained in more detail in Chapter 11.

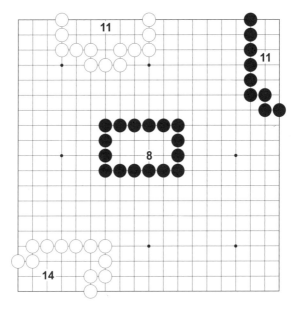

Diagram 10

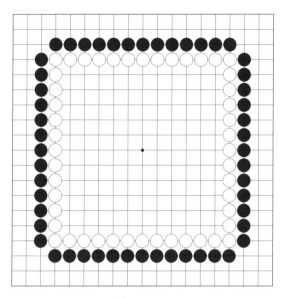

Diagram 11

CHAPTER 4

Connection and Disconnection

The black and white stones are often likened to two opposing armies on a battlefield. When they are separated or cut off from their own lines they are more easily attacked and captured by the enemy.

Two or more stones of the same color can be connected into a single unit by placing them on intersections of vertical and horizontal lines. Connection is made diagonally only under certain conditions, as will be learned later. Look at Diagram 12, Figures A and B. All of the black stones are securely connected with each other. However, in the case of Figure C, the black stones are not connected. They have been cut off by White, and are in a disconnected position. Of course, the white stones in this situation are disconnected as well as the black.

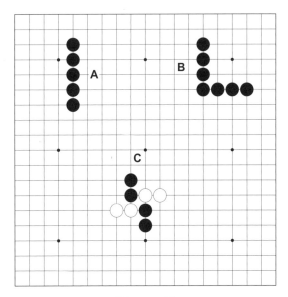

Diagram 12

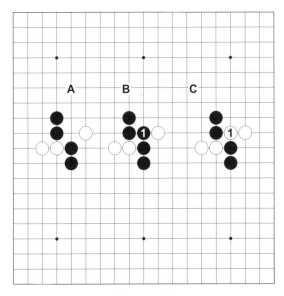

Diagram 13

Diagrams 13 and 14 illustrate how connection and disconnection may actually occur. In Diagram 13, if Black plays 1 as shown in Figure B, all the black stones will be connected. However, if it is White's turn to play and he plays 1 as indicated in Figure C, all the black stones will be disconnected into two separate groups.

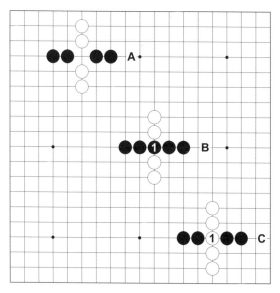

Diagram 14

In Diagram 14, where is the Black supposed to play in order to connect his own stones into a single unit?

There is no place to play other than 1 as indicated in Figure B. If White is to play first, on the contrary, he plays 1 just as Black did in Figure B and thus succeeds in disconnecting the black stones as indicated in Figure C.

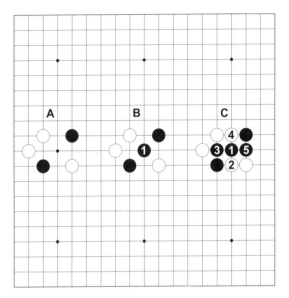

Diagram 15

Stones aligned diagonally are also considered as connected under certain conditions. Diagram 15 is an example of this situation. If Black is to play first, he plays 1 as indicated in Figure B and thus can connect his two stones. In this situation, there is no way for White to disconnect the black stones because the sequence thereof will be as shown in Figure C.

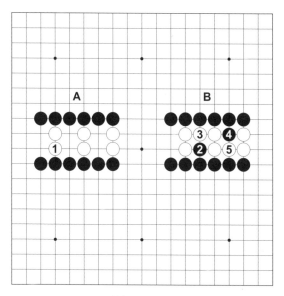

Diagram 16

Another example of stones not actually connected but which cannot be prevented from connecting can be seen in Diagram 16. In Figure B, White has connected diagonally by playing 3 and 5.

In the examples, play has been indicated on certain points of intersection. However, a little study will reveal that the same final situation will prevail regardless of which of the pertinent points of intersection is chosen for the first play.

In other words, any form of stones can be considered as connected if there is no way for either Black or White to effect disconnection by an alternate play.

CHAPTER 5

Capture

As briefly explained in Chapter 2, the player who so completely surrounds his opponent that no vacant point is left in the enclosure gains all the stones thus surrounded. Each stone captured is regarded as a penalty point to the value of one against the loser. When a player sees that capture of his stones is almost inevitable, he usually abandons for the moment the attempt to save them and plays at some more profitable point. Often by this method he is able to effect their rescue and even capture the attacking stones. Captured stones are called *hama*.

Diagram 17 shows the fundamental form of capture. As it stands in Figure A, the lone white stone is found in a position which will be completely surrounded by Black's next move. A stone or group of stones in this position is said to be in check. If it is Black's turn to play in this situation, he plays 1 as shown in Figure B and can capture and remove the one white stone from the board. Figure C shows the final position after the white stone was captured and removed from the board.

On the contrary, however, if White is to play first in the initial position, he plays 1 as indicated in Figure D and thereby escapes immediate capture.

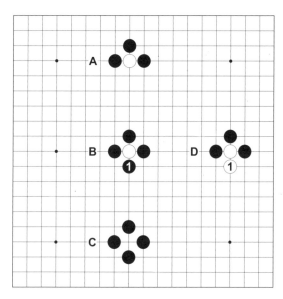

Diagram 17

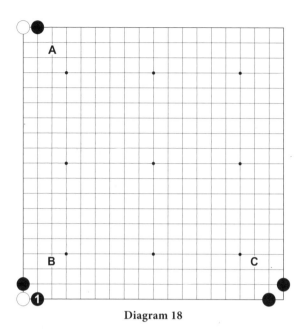

Diagram 18

A stone placed on the edge of the board is different in situation since the outer lines act as a boundary completing the enclosure. In the case of Diagram 18, if it is Black's turn to play, he plays 1 as shown in Figure B and thereby completes the enclosure, resulting in capture and removal of the white stone from the board. Figure C shows the position after the removal has taken place.

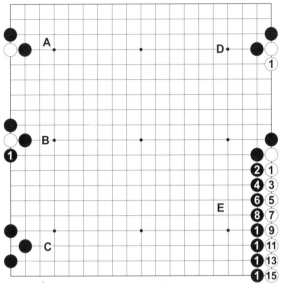

Diagram 19

Diagram 19 is similar in form to the one shown in Diagram 18. The lone white stone on the edge of the board in Figure A is in check as it stands. If it is Black's turn to play, he plays 1 as shown in Figure B and thereby can capture the one white stone (Figure C). Even if White is to play first as in Figure D, the result will be the same. White may extend along the line, but each move on the part of White will be followed by a corresponding pursuing move by Black as indicated in Figure E, capturing all the white stones upon reaching the corner of the board.

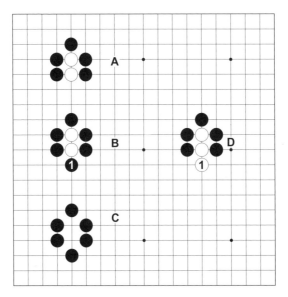

Diagram 20

In Diagram 20, Figure A, two white stones are in check. If Black plays 1 as shown in Figure B, he can capture the two white stones and remove them from the board. Figure C indicates the final position after removal. If, on the other hand, White is to play first, he must obviously extend at 1 as shown in Figure D, thereby escaping.

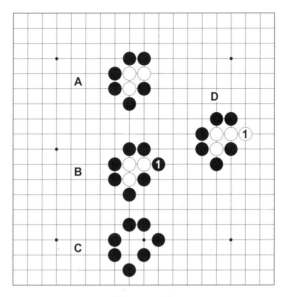

Diagram 21

In Diagram 21, Figure A shows a greater number of stones in check and how they are captured. The manner of play is exactly the same as the others previously explained. If Black plays 1 as shown in Figure B, he can capture the three white stones. Figure C is the final position. If, however, White has the first play, he can save the stones from capture by extending at 1 as in Figure D.

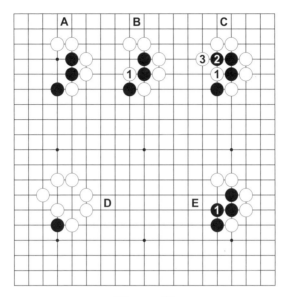

Diagram 22

The two black stones in Diagram 22, Figure A, are partly surrounded by White. If White plays first, Black cannot save his two
stones from capture. Figures B and C show the capturing process
and the final position after removal is shown in Figure D. On the
contrary, however, if Black plays first he can save his two stones by
connecting them to his outer stone as indicated in Figure E.

In Diagram 23, Figure A, if one black stone is cut off by White as shown therein, there is no way to defend it. Even if Black tries to escape by extending at 2 as in Figure B, capture is obvious, and the two black stones are removed from the board as in Figure C.

Therefore, if it is Black's turn to play, he plays 1 as shown in Diagram 24, Figure A and lets White take the one black stone, thereby acquiring his territory on the left side. If Black fails to do so, White usually extends his stones towards the corner as shown in Figure B without taking one black stone (it can be captured any time) and advances into Black's territory. Consequently, it must always be remembered that losses must be minimized.

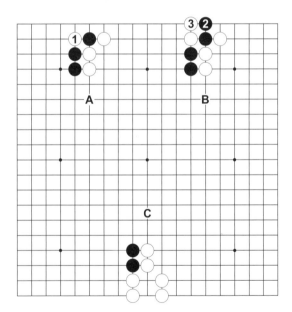

Diagram 23

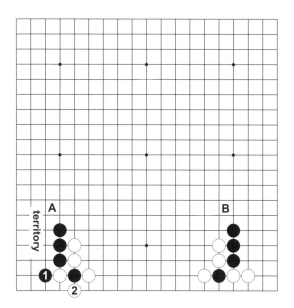

Diagram 24

Look at Diagrams 25 and 26. These are much more complicated situations concerning capture. If White plays correctly as indicated in the process of Diagram 25, he will be able to capture the black stones without fail, but if he plays as shown in Diagram 26, Black finds his way of escape and cannot be captured, resulting in figures as indicated. From these examples, study the direction in which to place your stones so as to prevent the opponent's escape. These tactics will be set forth in detail later.

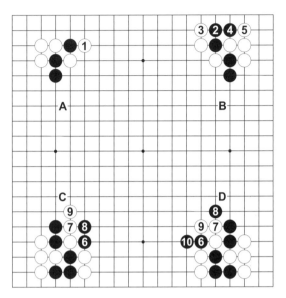

Diagram 25

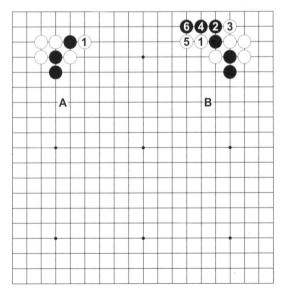

Diagram 26

CHAPTER 6
Life and Death

If a group of stones contains two or more separate "eyes" it is safe and cannot be captured, though it is completely surrounded by the opponent. The reason is that to play on any point which is completely surrounded by the opponent's stones is prohibited unless the play results in the capture of all or part of the surrounding stones. This is a result of the rule for surrounding and taking stones and not a separate rule. It follows necessarily from the method by which stones are captured. It is the most important principle of the game.

In order to understand the rule of the "eye," you must first examine the situation shown in Diagram 27, Figure A. The vacant point in the center of the white group is the eye which is called *me* in Japanese. However, any group of stones must have at least two eyes to be secure, and one eye alone is useless. For instance, if the white group in this diagram is completely surrounded by Black as shown in Figure B, the whole white group is killed by Black by playing at 1. Figure G shows the final position after the white group is removed from the board.

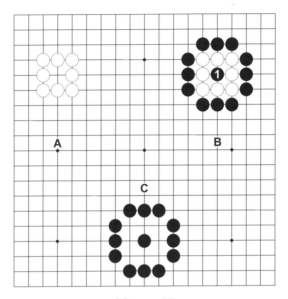

Diagram 27

Diagram 28 shows a safe group containing two separate eyes. The white group shown in Figure A is perfectly secure although it has been completely surrounded by the Black. The reason why the group is permanently safe is because even if a black stone could be played on *one* of the vacant intersections—"a" *or* "b"—there still remains one space yet to be filled in order to effect capture. The rule against playing on a point surrounded by the opponent's stones *unless capture can thereby be effected* is applicable and prevents this play. The black stone itself would be dead as soon as it touched the board, and hence it would be impossible to surround this group of white stones unless two stones were played at once. The white stones, therefore, cannot be surrounded or captured. This is the principle of the two eyes. In other words, a safe group is defined as the group of stones containing two vacant points on which play is forbidden.

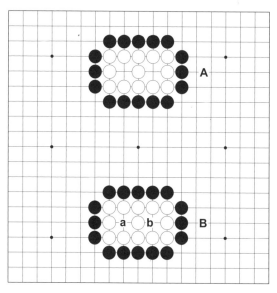

Diagram 28

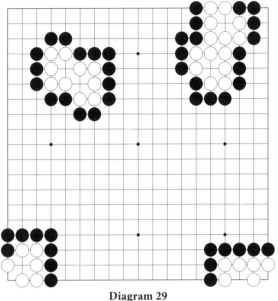

Diagram 29

Diagram 29 shows some other examples of safe groups of stones. Each of them contains two separate eyes and is perfectly secure at all times. It makes no difference whether the vacant eyes are situated on the edges or in the corners of the board or how far from each other they may be.

Beginners frequently form groups containing false eyes which are called *kageme. Kage* means "chipped" or "incomplete." By a false eye is meant a vacant point which must be occupied in order to prevent capture by the opponent's completion of a cordon at that point.

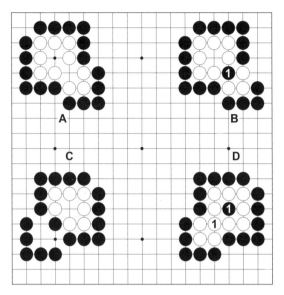

Diagram 30

Examine Diagram 30, Figure A. At a glance, this white group seems to have two eyes, but if you look at it carefully you can see that three white stones are in check since they are not connected to the remainder. If a black stone is played at 1 as shown in Figure B, it can capture three stones and remove them from the board, resulting in the situation shown in Figure C. The capture of the remaining white stones is obvious on the next move. Even if the White tries to defend his three white stones by playing at 1 as shown in Figure D, on the next play Black at 2 can capture all the white stones.

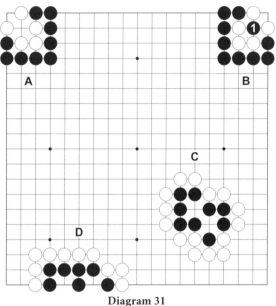

Diagram 31

Diagram 31, Figures A and B are further examples of this kind. Both white groups are dead. In Figure A, the three white stones are in check. Black can kill them by playing 1 as shown in Figure B. The Black groups shown in Figures C and D are also dead. One black stone is in check in each case, and if Black desires to defend it from capture he has to connect it to the main group. The group is thus reduced to a one-eyed group.

In actual games there are often groups of stones that at first glance seem to have two true eyes but are really open to attack. Frequently beginners find it hard to distinguish a real eye from a false eye.

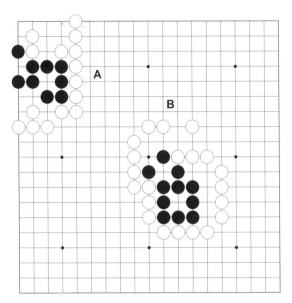

Diagram 32

The Black groups shown in Diagram 32 are dead although they have not yet been completely surrounded because they have only one real eye as they stand and there is no way for them to escape from the cordon of the opponent. In these cases, it is not necessary for White to fill up the vacant spaces in order to remove them from the board. They are regarded as dead before they are surrounded completely, and White can take them off the board at the end of the game without filling up those vacant intersections.

Life or death of a group of stones depends upon which player is to play first.

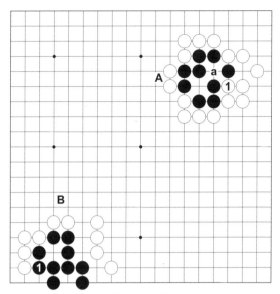

Diagram 33

In the situation shown in Diagram 33, Figure A, if it is White's turn to play and he plays 1, he can kill the black group of stones since the point "a" is false. If, on the other hand, it was Black's turn, he could save his group by playing at the same place.

Figure B merely shows another example of the same situation. Depending upon which side plays first, the whole black group of stones can or cannot be saved. If Black plays first, the life of the group is obviously saved by playing at 1 as indicated.

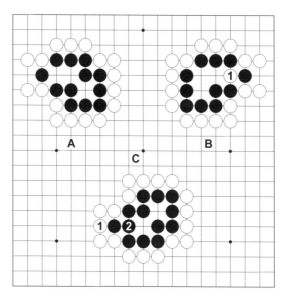

Diagram 34

Look at Diagram 34 carefully. This is to show how you can kill a group of stones by rendering the group hopeless because of a false eye. Where do you have to play in order to kill the black group of stones in this diagram?

The play at 1 as shown in Figure B is correct, and you can, in so doing, kill the whole group because the point at 1 is a false eye. However, if, by mistake, you play at 1 as indicated in Figure C, you can never kill this group because it now has two separate eyes by Black playing at 2.

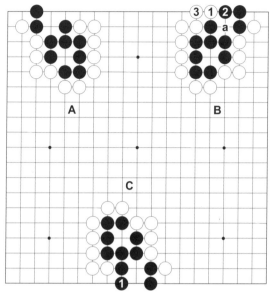

Diagram 35

Diagram 35 is another example of a false eye. All of the black stones will be killed if White is to play first, although at first sight this may not be apparent. The proper sequence of play for White is as shown in Figure B ("a" is false). If, on the other hand, it is Black's turn, he can save his group by playing at 1 as indicated in Figure C.

There is another important rule you must learn about the life or death of a group of stones.

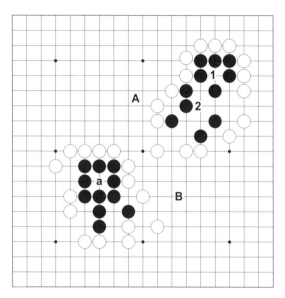

Diagram 36

Groups of stones which contain vacant spaces can be lost or saved depending on whether or not two separate eyes can be formed in those spaces. Diagram 36, Figure A, is an example of this. The point marked "1" is a real eye, and you can definitely make another eye at the point marked "2." Figure B shows a hopeless group of stones which cannot form an additional eye. It contains one real eye as it stands but there is no possibility of forming another. This can be proved by studying the previous example shown in Diagram 33. The group can make nothing but a false eye.

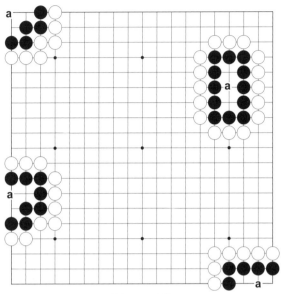

Diagram 37

The four black groups in Diagram 37 can form two separate eyes if Black plays first at the points marked "a." If, on the contrary, White plays first, he can kill these groups by playing at the same point.

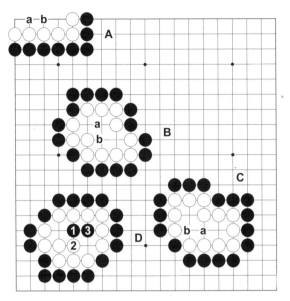

Diagram 38

To test your understanding thus far, try to solve the situation in Diagram 38, Figure A, before reading further.

White is safe even though Black plays first in this situation. If Black enters at "a," White saves by playing at "b"; if Black plays at "b," White plays at "a" and thus has two eyes. Figures B and C show you the same situations as this. In both situations shown therein, if Black plays at "a," White plays at "b"; if Black plays at "b," White plays at "a" and thus makes two separate eyes. You now understand clearly that these white groups cannot be killed even if Black plays first. However, the situation shown in Figure D is quite different from the previous situations. If it is Black's turn to play, he can kill the white group by playing at 1. If White plays at 2, Black plays at 3, thus rendering White hopeless to make two eyes. If White can play first, White can play to 1, thus making two eyes.

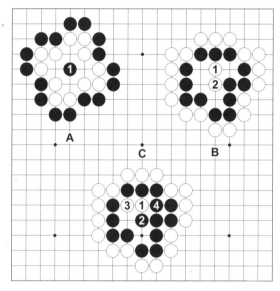

Diagram 39

A few more examples are shown in Diagram 39. In Figure A, if Black plays at 1, he can kill the white group, while White to the same point would form four eyes. Figure B is a position somewhat similar to the last. If White plays at 1 and is permitted to follow with 2, then Black cannot be saved. Therefore, upon White's playing at 1, Black must at once play at 2, thereby being able to defend his group. If White continues to play at 3 as indicated in Figure C, Black simply joins at 4 and is safe.

There exist many more types of "safe and dead" groups of stones other than those shown and explained in this chapter. However, it is very hard to master all of them in a short period of time. It is suggested that you make progress by study or by seeking the assistance of an advanced player. The knowledge acquired through close study of the examples shown in this chapter will illustrate the principle and will prove of immeasurable value.

CHAPTER 7
Illegal Plays

In Chapter 2, you learned that you may play on any vacant point of intersection of the board which you desire to occupy except as stated in Rule 6. However, there are some illegal plays which are exceptions.

Rule 6 provides that neither player is permitted to place a stone on a point that is completely surrounded by the opponent if there is only the one point vacant, unless that play results in the capture of some of the surrounding stones. In other words, it is forbidden to place any stone in a position which deprives it of liberty.

In Diagram 40, Figures A, B, and C, White is forbidden to play at the one remaining vacancy because all of these plays leave the white stones involved without liberty. For the very same reason, Black is forbidden to play on the center of the white group D.

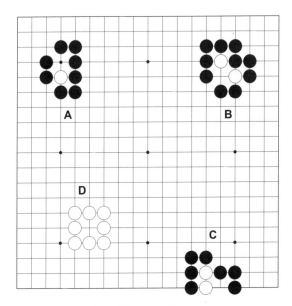

Diagram 40

However, Diagram 41 illustrates that White can play on a point that was forbidden in the preceding diagram because if he does this he can capture part or all of the black stones and also obtain a liberty for his stone. The results of such play are seen in Diagram 42.

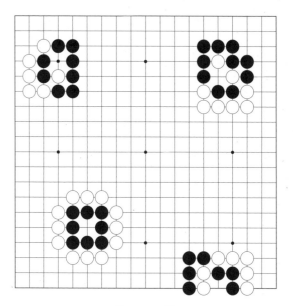

Diagram 41

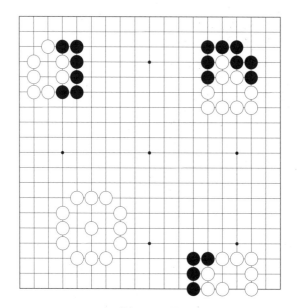

Diagram 42

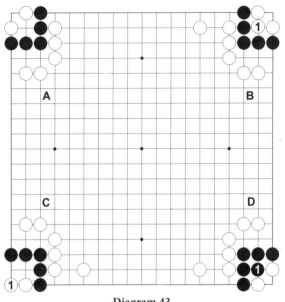

Diagram 43

In Diagram 43, Figure A, if it is White's turn to play, he can prevent Black from making two eyes by playing as indicated in Figures B or C. If, on the other hand, it is Black's play, he can save his group by playing at 1 as in Figure D, for it is now impossible for White to play on the corner. Of course, Black can play on the corner since he then captures two white stones.

CHAPTER 8

SEKI Situation

It is now time to study the situation called *seki* which may be translated as "a neutral position."

It sometimes happens that a series of plays will develop into an impasse or draw, and, when this occurs, the area involved is neutralized, ignored, and omitted from scoring calculations.

Such positions as are shown in Diagram 44 demonstrate *seki* situations. It may be seen that neither side can enter without at once losing stones on the next move of the opponent. However, the outer walls being open to attack, there always exists the chance of their being captured. In that case, the *seki* situation is broken up and capture effected in the usual way.

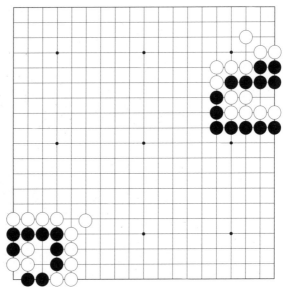

Diagram 44

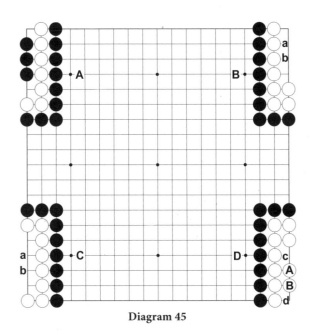

Diagram 45

Diagram 45, Figure A, shows another *seki* situation. If Black in this situation plays at either one of the two vacant points, White captures four black stones as shown in Figures B and C, subsequently making the necessary two eyes by playing either at "a" or "b." If Black plays at "a," White must play at "b," otherwise Black will do so and eventually capture all of the white stones. In order to capture them, the following steps are used. Black plays either at "c" or "d" as shown in Figure D, and then White captures three black stones because the white group is in check. Black plays again, placing a stone upon the middle point of three left vacant so as to prevent two separate eyes in the white group.

Here are some other examples of *seki* position. In both situations shown in Diagram 46, Figures A and B, neither can attack the other without risking certain death. All vacant points inside the surrounding walls are regarded as neutral territories which cannot be counted or claimed by the players. There are, of course, many *more* seki situations but by now you should generally understand what they are and recognize those which may occur in actual games.

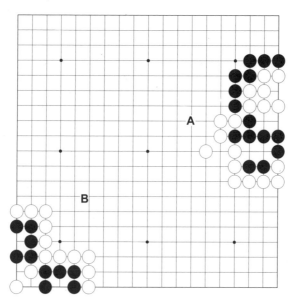

Diagram 46

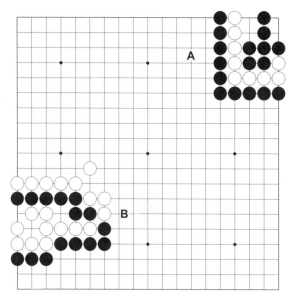

Diagram 47

However, the situation shown in Diagram 47, Figure A is quite different from those previously shown although this may not be apparent to you. It is clearly seen that the black group has an eye on the corner but the white group doesn't. The position is now no longer *seki,* but is called by the Japanese *me ari me nashi,* or literally "having an eye, not having an eye." In this case, the white stones are dead because if Black plays at either one of two adjacent vacant points, White cannot kill the black stones by playing at the remaining vacancy, for the reason that the vacant eye is still left vacant. Figure B merely shows another example of this.

CHAPTER 9

KO Situation

There is one exception to the rule that players may place their stones on any vacant points of intersection. This rule is called *ko* and is one of the most interesting features of the game. An example is shown in Diagram 48.

Assuming that it is White's turn to play, he can play 1 as shown in Figure A and can take the one black stone which is already surrounded on three sides, and the position shown in Figure B would then result. It is now obvious that the white stone which has just been played is surrounded by three black stones. If, as in Figure C, Black captures this white stone, we are back to the position we started with in Figure A. If the players were permitted to take stones by repeating moves in this way, the game would be endless. In order to allow the game to continue, the following rule was established when a player has captured an enemy stone in a *ko* position, his opponent may not recapture until he first makes at least one play elsewhere on the board.

This rule not only prevents the above situation but it also adds interest to the play. When a player is thus prevented from retaking a stone, he tries to play in another area where he can attack a larger group of stones than is involved in the situation where *ko* occurs. In this way he forces his opponent to follow him, after which he can return to retake the stone in *ko*.

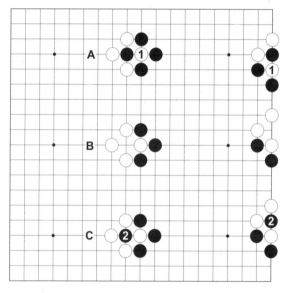

Diagram 48

The three examples on the right in Diagram 48 show the same situation as previously mentioned. In this elementary *ko* situation, there is but one stone involved. However, in actual games the outcome of a *ko* fight concerns the life or death of large groups of stones and often decides the results of the game.

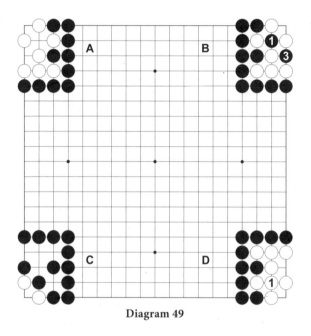

Diagram 49

In the situation shown in Diagram 49, Figure A, if it is Black's turn to play, he will undoubtedly play 1 as shown in Figure B and thereby capture the white stone in *ko*. Four white stones are in check. Although it is now White's turn, he is not permitted to retake the black stone immediately but he must first play somewhere else on the board. If Black on his next move, regardless of where White may have played, captures the four white stones in check by playing at 3, the resulting position will be as indicated in Figure C. He has thus acquired territory valued at a total of 15 points as indicated in the following computation: (Eight points indicate captured intersections.)

8 points plus 5 captured stones plus 2 dead stones equals 15 points.

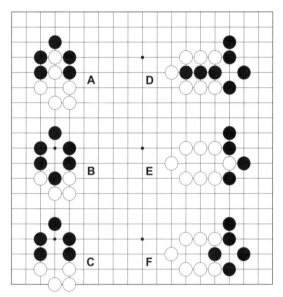

Diagram 50

As you learned in the previous chapter, these captured stones are used to fill up the vacant spaces claimed by the opponent, and, therefore, each of those stones is counted as 1 point. It is needless to say that the two dead stones which are left in the corner can be removed from the board at the end of the game.

On the contrary, however, if White can play first in the situation shown in Figure A, he can doubtless fill in *ko* with the play as shown in Figure D and thereby form two separate eyes, making his group of stones permanently safe from attack.

A situation which sometimes is mistaken for *ko* occurs when a player takes more than one stone and the stone thus played is threatened on three sides. In this case, the opponent retakes at once because it is obvious that an endless series of moves will not ensue.

Diagram 50 illustrates this. In the example shown in Figure A, Black can take two white stones with the results indicated in Figure B. In this case, White can immediately retake the one black stone as in Figure C for the reason above mentioned. A similar situation is shown in Figures D, E, and F for your study. It should not be difficult for you to understand these examples.

CHAPTER 10

Basic Tactics

Inasmuch as go is a game of strategy, in which there are many tactical procedures, it is necessary for beginners to learn at least some of the fundamental basic tactics. You should be able to master them without much difficulty if you remember what you have learned in the previous chapters.

Set forth below are some of the tactics needed to meet situations that develop during play.

In Diagram 51 it is Black's play and he must play at 1, whereupon White attempts to live by playing at 2. Black has to play at 3, and the subsequent steps are taken as recorded. This results in the capture of the white stones upon reaching the edge of the board. This situation is called *shicho* which means "a running attack."

Therefore when such a position develops a shrewd player would not extend his losses in this way but would instead play elsewhere, abandoning temporarily the threatened stone.

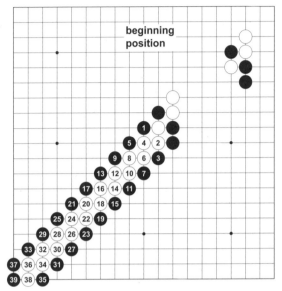

Diagram 51

On the other hand, however, the case is not hopeless if there is a friendly stone in the line of flight, no matter how far off it may be. This stone is called *shicho atari,* which may be translated as "a stone of refuge from a running attack." A study of Diagram 52 shows the truth of this. As you can see, Black cannot capture the white stones in a *shicho,* because the threatened white stones are eventually connected with the stone of refuge as shown in Figure B. The single white stone marked as 1 in Figure A is the stone of refuge.

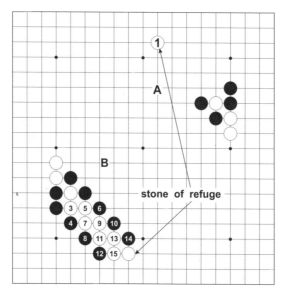

Diagram 52

If Black fails to notice the meaning of this white stone and plays at some other place on the board, White immediately attempts to escape by playing at 3 and eventually succeeds in connecting to the white single stone above mentioned. In this situation Black should not have tried to capture the white stone in this manner because now his own stones are in a position to be attacked by White in many directions.

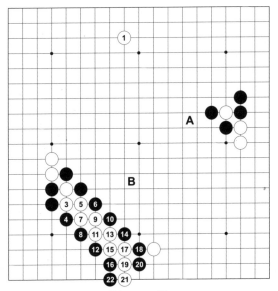

Diagram 53

In the situation shown in Diagram 53, Figure A, the waiting white stone is not posted on the line of progress, in which case the running attack is successful as indicated in Figure B. White must be careful not to misplace the stone of refuge in an attempt to escape from the running attack.

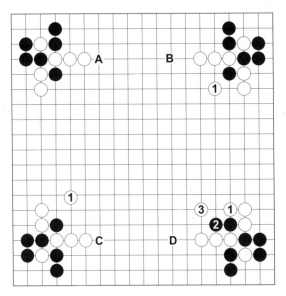

Diagram 54

There are many ways for White to prevent the black stone from escape in Diagram 54, Figure A. The plays in Figures B and C are correct and these plays are called *geta,* which may be translated as "capping" plays. Figure D is a *shicho* which you have already learned: if Black tries to escape by playing at 2, White, needless to say, plays at 3, a capping play.

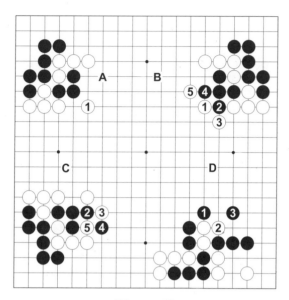

Diagram 55

Diagram 55 is another example of a capping play. In this situation, there is no possibility for Black to find a way to escape. Figures B and C show you the truth of this.

Similar cases frequently occur in actual games. If you memorize these plays, you will find no difficulty in preventing the escape of your opponent's stones.

Another example of a capping play is shown in Figure D, and from this example you should learn why the Black at 1 and 3 are essential in order to prevent the flight of the hostile stone.

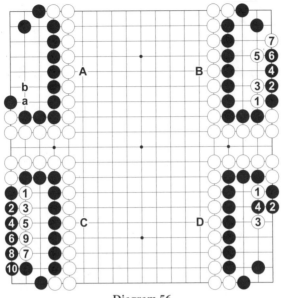

Diagram 56

In the situation shown in Diagram 56, Figure A, Black must make an additional play either at "a" or "b" in order to defend his territory completely. If Black fails to do so, the one black stone will be captured by a capping play as shown in Figure B, resulting in a big loss of Black's territory. Figures C and D show two incorrect plays for White, in which cases Black loses nothing and, on the contrary, the white stones are dead.

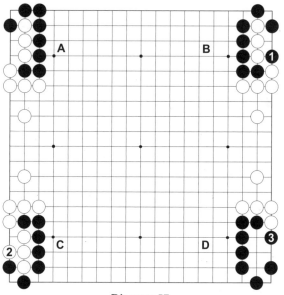

Diagram 57

In the situation shown in Diagram 57, Figure A, if it is Black's turn to play, he must play 1 as in Figure B, thus threatening the three white stones. White may reply by playing at 2 and captures the one black stone previously placed as indicated in Figure C, but Black will again play at 3 (the same point as played in Figure B) and he captures the four white stones as in Figure D since they have been completely enclosed by White's last move. Black's play is called *uttegae* which means "sacrifice play." It is incorrect for Black to play at 1 as in Diagram 58, Figure A, for then White promptly joins by playing at 2 as in Figure B, threatening the two black stones. If Black attempts to save them by playing at 3 as in Figure C, White can capture the four black stones by playing at "a."

If, on the other hand, it is White's turn to play in the initial situation, he must play 1 as shown in Figure D, thus preventing capture as indicated in Diagram 57.

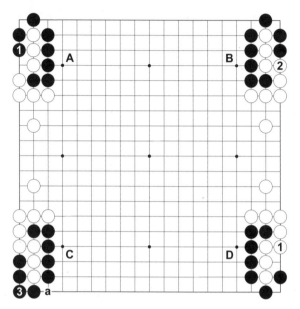

Diagram 58

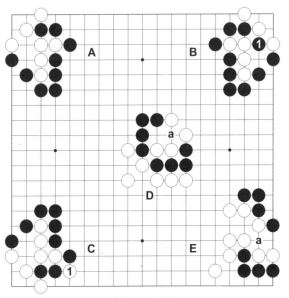

Diagram 59

Diagram 59 shows another example of sacrifice play. If it is Black's turn to play in this situation, he plays 1 as indicated in Figure B and the four white stones are in check. If White plays as shown in Diagram 57 and captures the one sacrifice black stone, Black re-enters and captures the five which are enclosed. The remaining three need not be removed though they are dead; they can be taken off the board at the end of the game. On the contrary, if White can play first, he plays 1 as in Figure C, capturing the two black stones. He can now make the necessary eyes with little difficulty.

Two more examples of these situations are shown in Figures D and E. If it is Black's turn to play in these situations, he plays at the point marked "a" and thereby captures the two white stones. On the contrary, if White can play first, he can save his two stones by playing at the same point.

In the situation shown in Diagram 60, all three white stones will be killed if it is Black's turn to play. Black plays 1. White tries to escape by playing at 2. Black then plays at 3, and now the four white stones are in check. White attempts to avoid capture by playing at 4, capturing one black stone. Black continues by playing at 5, again threatening. If White fills the point at "a," Black can capture all the seven white stones. This position is called *tsuru no sugomori*, which literally means "the confinement of cranes to their nest."

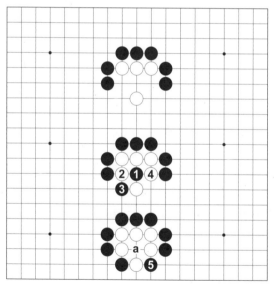

Diagram 60

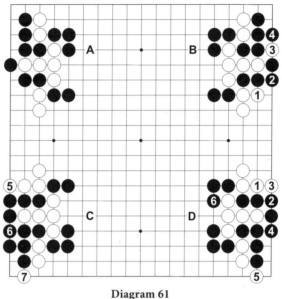

Diagram 61

If it is White's turn to play in Diagram 61, Figure A, how can he save his five stones? The correct method is shown in Figures B and C. White must check two black stones first by playing at 1 and Black then connects with 2. The next move of White is important. He must pitch in a stone at 3 and let Black capture it with 4. White then checks four black stones by playing at 5, and if Black attempts to avoid capture by connecting at 6, White gives a check at 7. It is now easily seen that there is no way for Black to escape capture. However, if White neglects to sacrifice a stone as he did in Figure B, he accomplishes nothing but loses his own five stones as in Figure D.

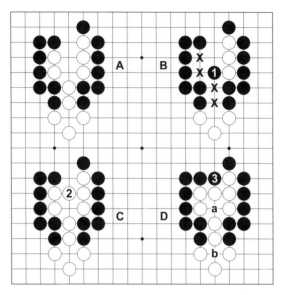

Diagram 62

Diagrams 62 and 63 show two more examples of sacrifice plays. In the situation shown in Diagram 62, Figure A, if it is Black's turn to play, he must sacrifice a stone by playing at 1 as shown in Figure B, and now the four white stones marked "X" are in check. White attempts to avoid capture by playing at 2 as in Figure C, capturing the one black stone. Black then threatens the six white stones by playing at 3 as in Figure D. If White fills the point at "a," Black can capture the nine white stones on his next move at "b." If however, White can play first in the original situation, he can save them by playing at the same point as Black did in Figure B because he can now connect at the point marked "b" whenever threatened.

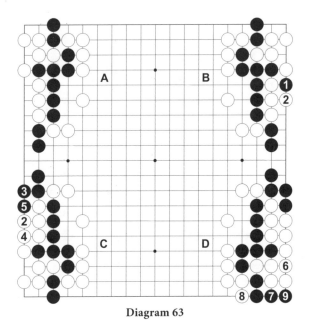

Diagram 63

In the situation shown in Diagram 63, Figure A, if it is Black's turn to play, he can save his seven stones, which seem to be unable to escape from the cordon of the white group, by playing as follows. First Black must play 1, threatening the one white stone. White replies with 2 and captures the one black stone. Black then plays 3. If White, on his next move, replies by playing at 4 in order to save his four stones, Black then plays at 5 and thereby threatens the six white stones. If White connects them with his comrade by playing at 6, Black can capture the eleven white stones by playing at 7 and 9 as shown in Figure D.

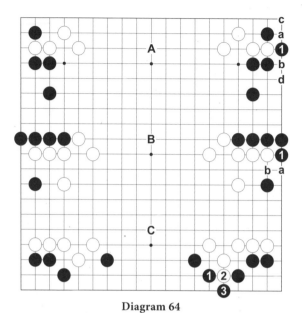

Diagram 64

Diagram 64 shows some joining methods on the edge of the board. In each illustration, if Black plays 1, he can join his two groups of stones. Black's play at 1 is called *watari*, which literally means "crossing over."

Let's examine each situation in detail and ascertain why White cannot break Black's joining after playing at 1. In the situation shown in Figure A, if White plays either "a" or "b," he will be immediately killed by Black at "c" or "d." In Figure B, if White attempts to advance by playing at "a," Black replies with "b," if White plays "b," Black then replies with "a." In Figure C, if White tries to advance by playing at 2, Black can avoid it by playing at 3. White henceforth cannot break Black's connection because of the reason shown in Figure A.

CHAPTER 11
Playing the Game

As you have completed a study of the rules, tactics, and objectives of go, you are now ready to learn some of the game's mechanics.

The game is commenced by playing in or around the corners of the board. The reason for this, as has been pointed out, is that the corners are the easiest areas in which to form territory and the simplest to defend. The next most advantageous sections are the sides, while the center of the board is the most difficult area in which to form territory. This fact is sufficiently proved by the figures shown in Diagram 65. Each of the groups has surrounded twelve points of territory. However, you will quickly observe that these territories have not been formed with the same number of stones:

Corner	————————	8 stones
Side	————————	12 stones
Center	————————	18 stones

Obviously, it is easier to form territory in the corners of the board than any other place. Such being the case, in an ordinary game the play generally proceeds from the corners and edges to the center. However, other factors than the acquisition of territory must be considered. Maneuverability towards the center is one of them. Nevertheless, the principle illustrated in Diagram 65 is a basic fundamental of the game.

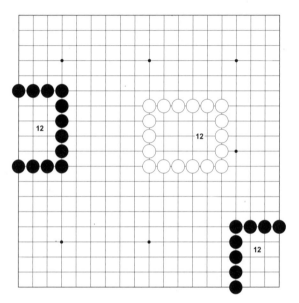

Diagram 65

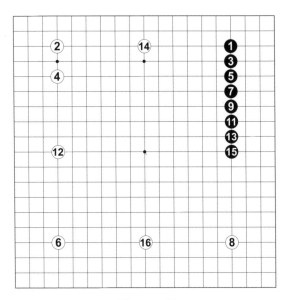

Diagram 66

Study Diagram 66 and you will note that Black with his first plays up to 15 has sequestered about 30 points of territory. But while he was devoting himself to one specific territory, White has ranged widely over the rest of the board with a potential area worth many times the amount of territory acquired by Black. This indicates that you must pay attention to the entire board, and it is wise to outline loosely your desired territories in the beginning.

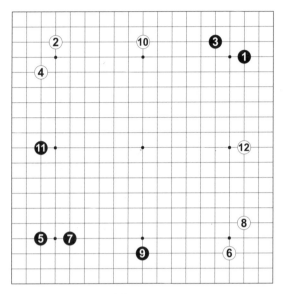

Diagram 67

Diagram 67 shows an example of correct opening procedure, although there are many other ways actually used at this stage of the game. The players moved first toward the corners where they either protected their corner or prevented the opponent from fortifying a corner.

There are several fundamental ways to play in or around the corners and Diagram 68 shows some of these. A stone placed on the intersection of the third and fourth lines from the edge of the board is called *komoku* in Japanese and it is the most flexible of all corner placements. Generally, three major methods are used for corner placements with *komoku*. Black's play at 1 shown in Figure A is called *keima* or *kogeima* which is similar to the knight's move in chess. This placement is called *kogeima shimari*. If the stones are one point farther apart as shown in Figure B, it is called *ogeima* which means "the great knight's move." The placement illustrated in Figure C is called *ikken shimari*. *Ikken* means "skipping one point."

Figure D shows a corner placement from the stone on the intersection of the fourth line from both edges of the board. You can also play at "a" or "b" as in the foregoing figures.

The opening play of the game is very important, however, and in order to acquire adequate knowledge of this, actual playing experience is necessary. It is not the purpose of this introductory book to teach the more complicated strategy. A careful study of the foregoing fundamentals will enable the interested reader to enjoy the ancient game of go and lead him to further study.

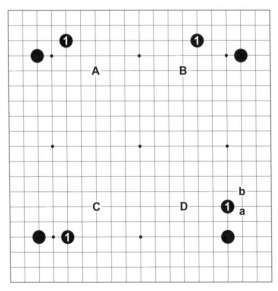

Diagram 68

Problems

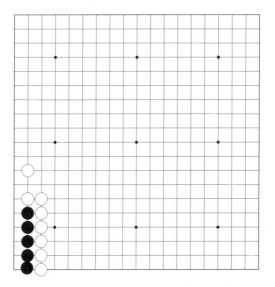

Problem 1 White to play. How can Black group be killed?

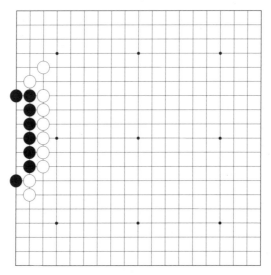

Problem 2 White to play. How can Black group be killed?

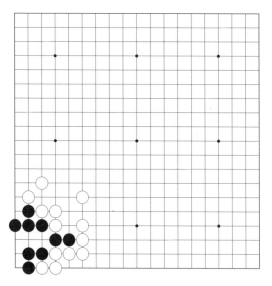

Problem 3 White to play. How can Black group be killed?

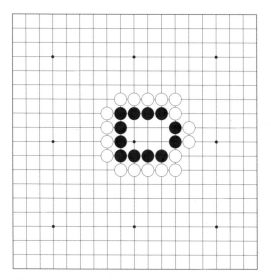

Problem 4 White to play. How can Black group be killed?

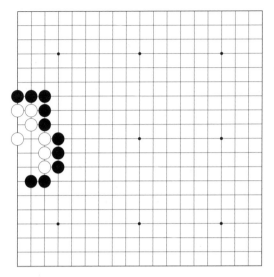

Problem 5 Black to play. How can White group be killed?

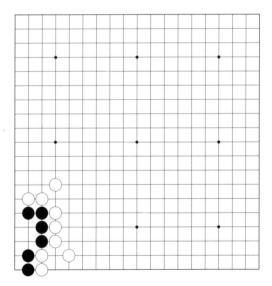

Problem 6 White to play. How can Black group be killed?

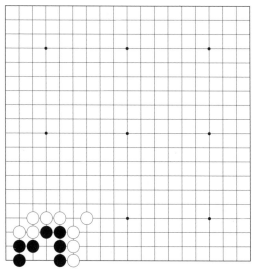

Problem 7 White to play. How can Black group be killed?

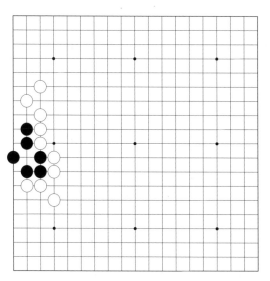

Problem 8 White to play. How can Black group be killed?

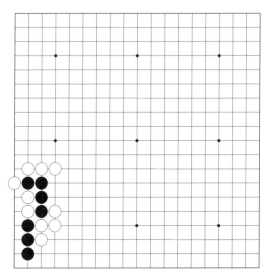

Problem 9 Black to play. The four black stones have only one escape from this trap. What is it?

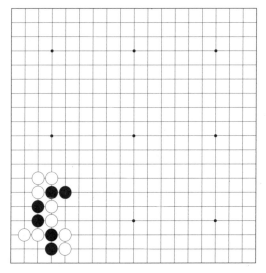

Problem 10 Black to play. Three disconnected Black groups can be connected by capturing some White stones. How?

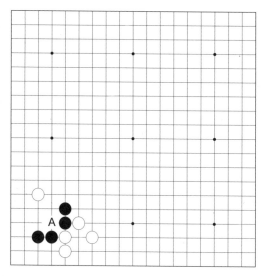

Problem 11 Black to play. How can White stone "A" be captured ?

(It cannot be taken by *shicho*.)

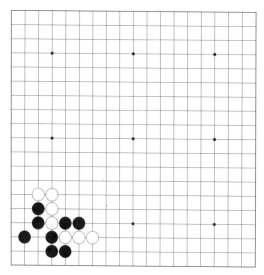

Problem 12 White to play. Two Black stones can be captured. How?

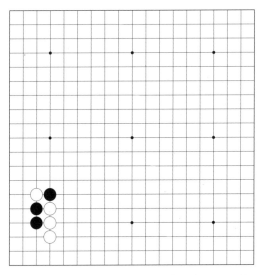

Problem 13 Black to play. How can the single White stone be captured?

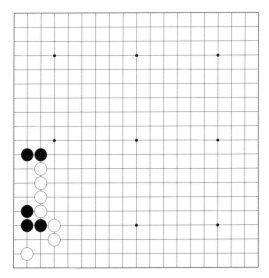

Problem 14 Black to play. How can the three Black stones
in the corner be connected with the other group?

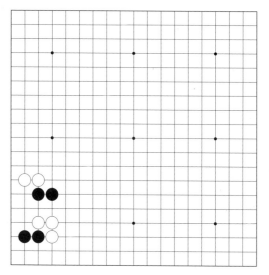

Problem 15 Black to play. How can the two Black groups be connected?

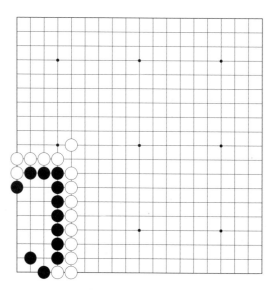

Problem 16 White to play. Black's corner territory
is still incomplete. How can it be broken up?

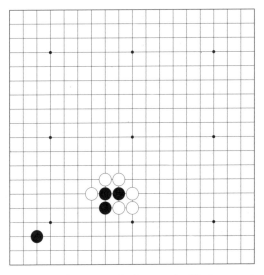

Problem 17 White to play. Using shicho, can the Black stones be captured?

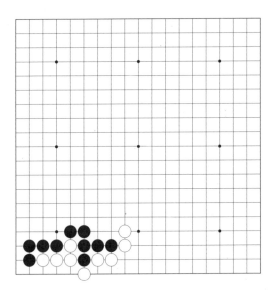

Problem 18 Black to play. The four White stones
on the corner can be captured. How?

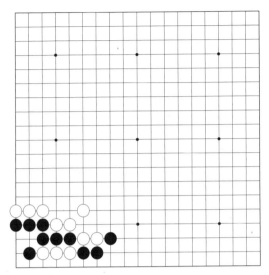

Problem 19 White to play. Three White stones are in danger. Using sacrifice play, they can be saved by capturing the Black stone on the corner. How?

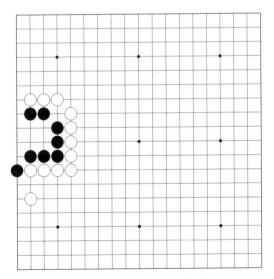

Problem 20 Black to play. How can the Black group be saved?

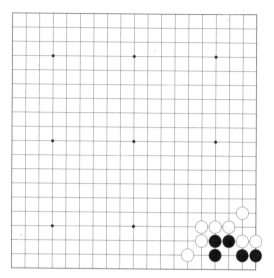

Problem 21 White to play. How can the Black group be killed?

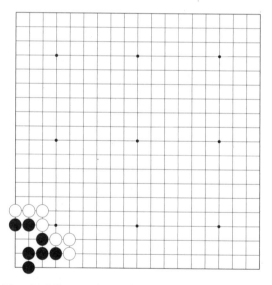

Problem 22 White to play. How can the Black group be killed?

Solutions

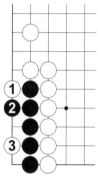

Solution 1 (a)

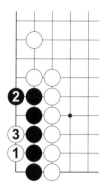

Solution 1 (b)

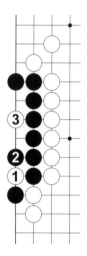

Solution 2 (a)

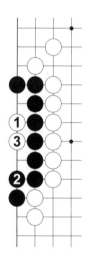

Solution 2 (b)

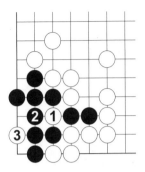

Solution 3 (a)

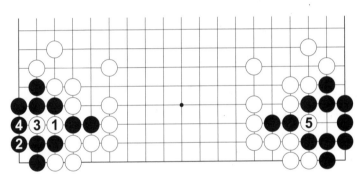

Solution 3 (b)

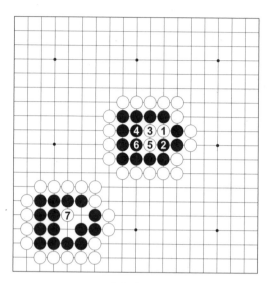

Solution 4

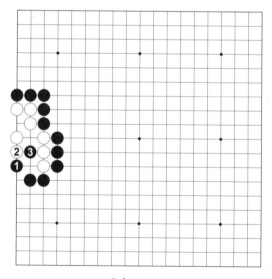

Solution 5

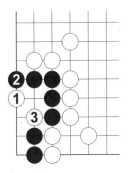

Solution 6 (a)

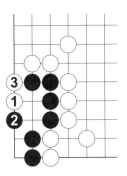

Solution 6 (b)

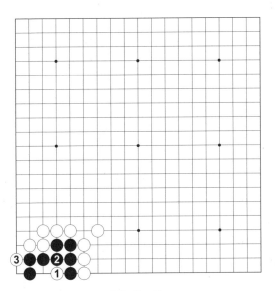

Solution 7

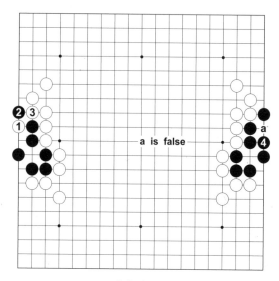

Solution 8

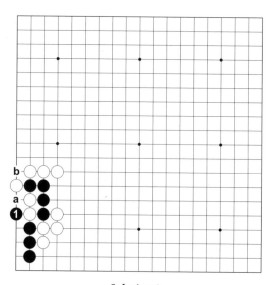

Solution 9

If White plays "a," all four stones can be captured when Black plays "b."

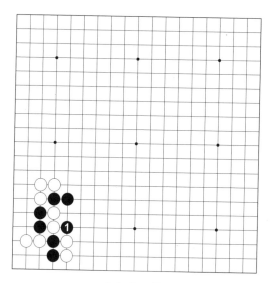

Solution 10

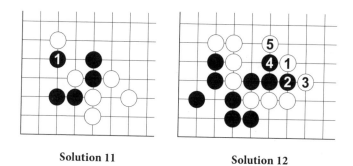

Solution 11

Solution 12

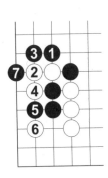

Solution 13

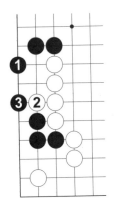

Solution 14

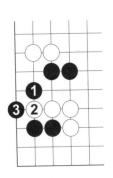

Solution 15

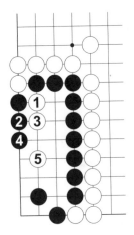

Solution 16

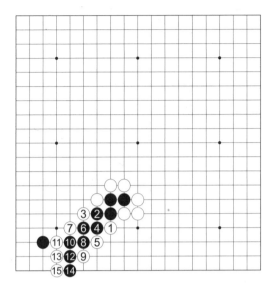

Solution 17

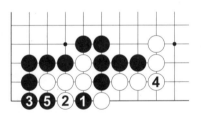

Solution 18 (a)

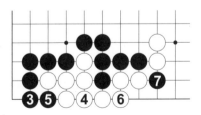

Solution 18 (b)

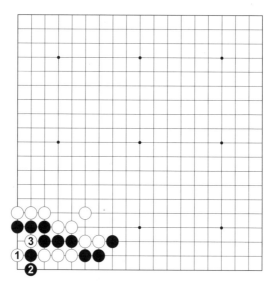

Solution 19

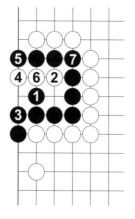

Solution 20 (a)

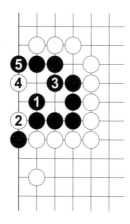

Solution 20 (b) *Seki*

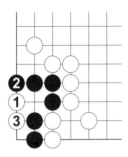

Solution 21 (a) White's play at 1 is the place to kill Black

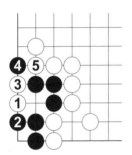

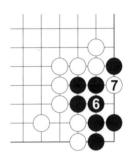

Solution 21 (b)

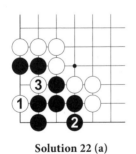

Solution 22 (a)

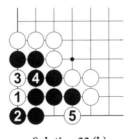

Solution 22 (b)

The End of the Game

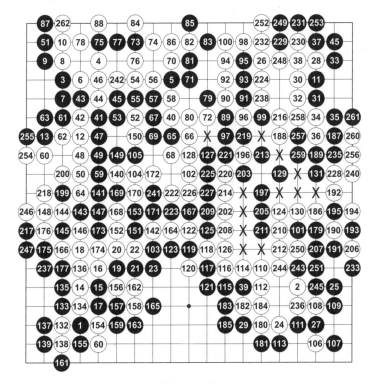

Diagram 69

The end of a game between a professional and a leading amateur

198 (white) 201 (black) and 204 (white) take *ko*

178 (white) was placed where 145 (black) is now

234 (white) was placed where 193 (black) is now, to terminate ko situation

239 (black) was placed where 96 (white) is now, to terminate ko situation

X = neutral territory filled in

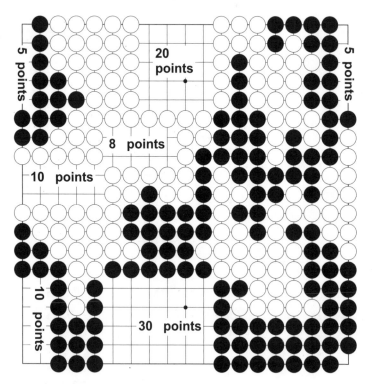

Diagram 70 A board arranged for counting purposes.